Confessing Faith

Confessing Faith

A Guide to Confirmation for Presbyterians

KATHY L. DAWSON

Geneva Press
Louisville, Kentucky

© 2006 Geneva Press

Scripture quotations from the New Revised Standard Version of the Bible are copyright © 1989 by the Division of Christian Education of the National Council of the Churches of Christ in the U.S.A. and are used by permission.

Book design by Sharon Adams
Cover design by Teri Vinson

First edition
Published by Geneva Press
Louisville, Kentucky

This book is printed on acid-free paper that meets the American National Standards Institute Z39.48 standard. ♾

PRINTED IN THE UNITED STATES OF AMERICA

06 07 08 09 10 11 12 13 14 15 — 10 9 8 7 6 5 4 3 2 1

Library of Congress Cataloging-in-Publication Data is on file at the Library of Congress, Washington, D.C.

ISBN-13: 978-0-664-50284-3
ISBN-10: 0-664-50284-9

Contents

CHAPTER 1

CONFIRMATION: WHAT IS IT?

The youth file into the pews of the church in their best attire. They look nervously around for friends and family members. They wonder: "Will I remember to say 'I do' and 'I will' in the right place?" "Will I be the only one without an elder sponsor or mentor here?" "Will I have to do anything in the front of the church that will embarrass me?" "Does this really mean anything anyway?"

The parents and guardians look on and remember when they first brought their son or daughter to this church or another for baptism or dedication. They wonder: "It seems like only yesterday and a lifetime ago." "Will my son stay in the church?" "Does my daughter really believe the things about her faith that are printed in this bulletin or read before the session?" "Does this really mean anything anyway?"

The minister and teacher beam at the youth, hoping to calm their fears so that all will go well in the service. They wonder: "Will they remember what we've just studied for eight weeks or a year?" "Are they joining the church for the 'right' reasons?" "Are they being pressured from home or their peers to do this without really desiring confirmation?" "Does this really mean anything anyway?"

The covenant partners look on with pride, remembering when they hardly knew these youth.[1] They remember tough faith conversations over pizza, working together to serve others, learning more about their own faith than they would have imagined. They wonder: "Will this friendship continue after this ceremony?" "For what will I pray for this youth?" "How will I continue to address the questions about my faith that were raised in this process?" "Does this really mean anything anyway?"

The rest of the congregation looks on and smiles. This act gives them hope that the church will continue beyond their time here. They wonder: "Who are these youth who stand before us?" "What will they contribute to the life of the church?" "Will we even see them around after this is over?" "Does this really mean anything anyway?"

An unobserved party looks on who has been with these youth since their life began. This being, for whom this worship act is performed, knows better than any of the previous parties what this step of commitment entails. Does God wonder about the relevance of this act of commitment to the other parties involved?

The minister begins: "We rejoice that you now desire to declare your faith and to share with us in our common ministry. In baptism you were joined to Christ, and made *members* of his church. In the community of the people of God, you have learned of God's purpose for you and for all creation. You have been nurtured at the table of our Lord, and called to witness to the gospel of Jesus Christ."[2]

> "We rejoice that you now desire to declare your faith and to share with us in our common ministry. In baptism you were joined to Christ, and made *members* of his church. In the community of the people of God, you have learned of God's purpose for you and for all creation. You have been nurtured at the table of our Lord, and called to witness to the gospel of Jesus Christ."

Exploring a Definition

What is this yearly moment of confirmation in the life of a congregation about? What is it about this event that evokes both wonder and puzzlement? In an age when Presbyterian Church membership is declining along with many of our sister denominations, does it really make a difference to enact this ancient ritual yet again?

These are some of the things I wonder about as the author of this book. I invite you, as reader, to explore with me the act of confirmation as it has been practiced in the church from its beginnings until now.

To begin we must first define what confirmation is and is not. Sometimes it is easier to begin with the "nots." We will look at three of these that inform our definition as Presbyterians:

- Confirmation is not a sacrament in and of itself.
- Confirmation is not simply a rite of passage.
- Confirmation is not simply becoming a church member.

Not a Sacrament

If you look for a confirmation service in the *Book of Common Worship* of the Presbyterian Church (U.S.A.) and the Cumberland Presbyterians, you will not be able to find one. In fact, you will not find the word *confirmation* in the table of contents at all. The words of the minister quoted above come from a service entitled, "Reaffirmation of the Baptismal Covenant for Those Making a Public Profession of Faith."

This is an indication of how Presbyterians view the act of confirmation. It is not sufficient in and of itself, but tied deeply to the act of baptism. Those seeking to join the early Christian fellowships would go through a process that would culminate in quick succession with baptism, confirmation, and Holy Communion in that order. If a confirmand (one desiring confirmation) has not been baptized as an infant or child, the act of baptism will directly precede the reaffirmation of baptism much as it occurred in early Christianity.

Presbyterians hold two sacraments: baptism and communion. What is a sacrament? *The Study Catechism: Confirmation Version*, of the Presbyterian Church (U.S.A.), defines it in this way: "A sacrament is a special act of Christian worship, instituted by Christ, which uses a visible sign to proclaim the promise of the gospel for the forgiveness of sins and eternal life. In baptism the sign is that of water; in the Lord's Supper, that of bread and wine."[3] The key words for our purposes here are, "instituted by Christ." From the Gospels we have evidence for Jesus requesting certain acts from his disciples. We find the mandate for baptism in the words of the Great Commission from the Gospel according to Matthew: "Go therefore and make disciples of all nations, baptizing them in the name of the Father and of the Son and of the

Holy Spirit" (Matt. 28:19). The request for communion is found within the act of Jesus Christ's last supper with his disciples before his arrest, as well as the words of Paul in 1 Corinthians 11:26: "For as often as you eat this bread and drink the cup, you proclaim the Lord's death until he comes."

Although Presbyterians hold to these two sacraments alone, other Christians—notably Roman Catholics—subscribe to seven sacraments by linking those acts instituted by Christ with those found in church tradition. For these Christians, confirmation is a sacrament with the visible sign of oil as its promise of the gospel. During the Reformation, Calvin and his followers, some of whom would become Presbyterians, reduced the number of sacramental acts to those mentioned specifically in the Gospels.

Not Simply a Rite of Passage

There is no standard age for confirmation, although many tie this act to the passage into adolescence or young adulthood. Many cultures have specific rituals around this passage. These ritual acts center around learning of group history and norms, testing of strength and abilities, differentiation of gender roles, and claiming a place in the community. They are very rich ceremonies commemorating a developmental passage, and may well be appropriate for general youth curriculum.[4] But they are not what informs the act of confirmation.

Confirmation is appropriate any time a baptized member expresses the desire to fully commit himself to a deepening relationship with God and to the work of the church. This may happen at other times than adolescence. It would be equally appropriate for an adult to commit herself to God and to the church through the confirmation process and a public profession of faith as it is for a youth. There are several reasons why most Presbyterian churches confirm early to middle adolescents. With infant baptism and the admittance of children to the Lord's Table, confirmation has moved to the time of adolescence and beyond as developmental life issues such as identity, questioning of previously held beliefs, and willingness to make a firm commitment come to the fore. Adolescence and young adulthood is a time of searching for something worthy of dedicating our lives to. We can only hope and pray that this passion is directed toward God and the church.

Another reason that confirmation is not strictly a rite of passage has to do with gender role training. In the Presbyterian Church (U.S.A.), all confirmed members may serve in the common ministry of the church. Women and men may become teachers, elders, deacons, and ministers. There may be times when gender specific curricula may be appropriate for youth, but confirmation's claim that we are all children of God does not make this distinction.

One other danger in linking the act of confirmation with a specific age and as a rite of passage is the implicit message that the preparation and training time in the confirmation process is leading to a ceremony akin to a graduation. Christian growth in faith is a lifelong process. It is not like middle school or high school in which a culmination ceremony indicates a departure from this particular educating community. Confirmation is in some sense more like a beginning than an ending. Even though God has been with us from birth, confirmation marks a taking up on our end of the promises made in this covenant relationship, promises that will take a lifetime to fulfill.

Not Simply Becoming a Church Member

Looking back at the final words of the minister at the beginning of this chapter, you may notice that the word *members* is emphasized. This emphasis is not my doing, but the way the words are printed in the *Book of Common Worship*. Membership is not linked to confirmation in the Presbyterian Church; it is found in the act of baptism. Even baptized infants are full members of the church! They probably will not be invited to serve on committees, to conduct a stewardship campaign, to sing in the choir, or to teach Sunday school, but they are members of the church nevertheless. It is this link between baptism and membership that prompted the Presbyterian Church to invite children to participate in the Lord's Supper whenever parents consider that their children sufficiently understand the meaning of the visible symbols of bread and wine as signs of Jesus Christ's presence and remembrance.

Confirmation will not change nonmembers into members of the church. In the baptismal service, both the congregation and the parents take vows. The vow of the congregation reads as follows: "Do you, as members of the church of Jesus Christ, promise to guide and nurture (these children) by word and deed, with love and prayer, encouraging them to know and follow Christ and to be faithful *members* of his church?"[5] Church members who understand this concept and take their baptismal vows seriously look for ways leading up to confirmation in which children can be active in the life of the congregation through service, worship participation, and study. What the confirmation process can do in its preparation is to help these already baptized members to identify their gifts and specific calling, which may inform their subsequent engagement in the common ministry of the church. Does a confirmand possess musical abilities, excel in the spiritual practice of hospitality, have great love for young children, delight in reading Scripture aloud? The diversity of God-given gifts may be evident in confirmation classes, in discussions with covenant partners as identified by parents and friends, and in the way that confirmands publicly express their faith. More will be said about nurturing these gifts beyond the act of confirmation in the final chapter of this book.

Confirmation: What It Is

We have spent some time looking at what confirmation is not. It is not a sacrament, a rite of passage, or a membership campaign. So what is it? In their book *Models of Confirmation and Baptismal Affirmation*, Robert Browning and Roy Reed offer eight different models or defining goals for the practice of confirmation as it is found in Christian churches today. The model which is closest to that practiced in the Presbyterian Church is "the affirmation of the baptismal covenant in adolescence or as a renewal of covenant at any time during life's pilgrimage when an individual comes to new or deepened understandings and/or commitments in faith."[6] This definition links confirmation to a reaffirmation of baptism, links confirmation to covenant language, and does not restrict it to a particular age. What is missing from this definition from a Presbyterian practice of confirmation is the importance of the public profession of faith. Those seeking confirmation in the Presbyterian Church are required to stand before the session and the congregation and state what they believe. Confirmation, then, may be defined as (a) *the reaffirmation of baptism* (b) *by a covenant commitment* (c) *through a public profession of faith*. Let's look at each of these in turn.

Reaffirmation of Baptism

Those who were baptized as infants remember little or nothing about this event. Some of the students I have taught in both confirmation classes and seminary classes have expressed disappointment that they don't remember their baptism, and that their friends from other traditions seem to have such vivid memories of this important event. It can be a rich experience to ask parents, family friends, and congregation members who were present at your baptism what that event was like. Many families do not regularly tell this story as they do other childhood stories.

Being too young to recall our baptism or to fully commit ourselves to a renunciation of evil and a turning to Jesus Christ, there comes a time when we must revisit these vows made on our behalf. Presbyterians do not believe in

rebaptizing a person, believing that the Holy
Spirit has already sealed and claimed the infant,
child, youth, or adult as a member of the
Christian church in their original baptism.
This is reflected in the way a reaffirmation service is conducted. A reaffirmation of baptism
consists of publicly answering the same questions made at our baptism, but does *not* use the
sign of water—whether sprinkled, poured, or
immersed—with the baptismal formula: "I bap-
tize you in the name of the Father, and of the
Son, and of the Holy Spirit."

To create a sensory reminder of baptism in
the midst of a reaffirmation service and to
strengthen the link between baptism and confirmation, some churches have found other means
of remembering the importance of the sign of
water. Some have poured water into the font
during the service. Others have had a small
fountain of continuously running water in place.
Some have placed pebbles in the font, inviting
participants and congregation members to take
a stone as they reaffirm their baptism. Some
have even dipped small tree branches into the
font and waved them high, sending water drops
on the whole congregation. All these practices
can create a deep sensory memory of confirmation as an act of reaffirmation of baptism.

As indicated in the Browning and Reed definition, this act of reaffirmation may be done more than once. As rich as a baptismal reaffirmation is during an adolescent confirmation process, it can occur at any age as one wants to mark a deepening commitment to God and turning away from sin and evil.

An Act of Covenant Commitment

This commitment is not done in isolation. Yes, there are certainly others present at the act of confirmation. We have mentioned some of them at the beginning of the chapter. They include the confirmands, parents or guardians (if youth), elder sponsors or mentors, and the pastors and teachers who have led the classes. There are also the visible people attending the service and the invisible host of saints who have paved the way with each individual to reach this particular moment.

The most important being, everpresent yet unseen, is the God who created each of the others. This God has invited all others present for this moment of confirmation since the beginning. God's covenant love extends beyond the bounds of the church walls to all of creation. The question becomes, if God has extended this invitation since birth, why does it take so long for us to respond, and why do we need training to say yes?

Why It Takes So Long to Respond

Has anyone ever extended an invitation to you that was difficult and life changing? Perhaps you were asked to serve as a class officer in school or to embark on a particular vocation that took extensive education and training. Perhaps you had a close friend who invited you into a romantic relationship, or someone from a different culture asked you to live in his or her community for an extended time. There are many other such invitations that take time to think about and commitment to undertake. There may also be barriers to accepting these invitations, such as time constraints, money matters, lack of interest, and other priorities. Some of these may seem beyond our control, but others revolve around our consistent inability to respond faithfully. This human tendency and condition is what Scripture and church tradition have called sin.

Included in the confirmation service is an ancient section called the "renunciations." There are several different versions of these questions in the *Book of Common Worship*. Churches at this time often search for the most pleasant and benign language to address the problems of sin and evil. Even though most Presbyterian services include a prayer of confession, we are tentative and careful in our language about this persistent human problem and

condition. Perhaps we are reacting to the fire
and brimstone preachers of the past who
damned their listeners because of their moral
failures. Perhaps we are embracing the pervasive
culture of consumerism and self-fulfillment at
any price. Perhaps we desire to emphasize God's
grace without remembering human sinfulness.
Dietrich Bonhoeffer pointed out the dangers of
such an emphasis in his concept of "cheap grace"
rather than "costly grace."

Whatever the reason, to accept the invitation
of God to covenant relationship, we must first
have our ears cleared to hear the call to confirmation and the response of Christian discipleship that this relationship requires. The early
church took seriously the power of sin and evil
in the course of the baptism/confirmation
process. Here is a description of the renunciation ritual during the time of Augustine
(354–430): "[Renunciation] involved a con-
temptuous hissing at baptismal candidates,
blowing all the evil out of their lives. As this took
place, the candidates stood without shoes on a
rough rag or animal skin, symbolizing the vices
on which they must learn to tread, and the first
clothing worn by Adam and Eve after their
expulsion from the garden."[7] Thankfully once
renouncing the power of sin and evil in our lives,
we can turn joyfully to life with Jesus Christ.

Why We Are Trained to Accept God's Invitation

Has anyone ever invited you to do something that you've never done before? For instance have you received an invitation to go bowling, ice skating, or hang gliding? Have you been asked to play an instrument, make a quilt, or teach a class? These activities and many others require training of some sort before one attempts them. Committing oneself to be a disciple of Christ requires even more training, because the invitation is not for a one-time event, but for a way of life.

Confirmation training takes on different forms in Presbyterian churches around the country. Some offer special classes at a time other than Sunday morning that may last anywhere from eight weeks to a year. Some offer the training during the regular Christian education program of the church and may consider their middle school or high school classes or new member classes as confirmation training. Many churches have apprenticeship or discipleship programs in addition to the group classes that allow confirmands to meet with an elder sponsor or mentor for individual conversation on faith issues and the meaning of a life committed to Christian discipleship.

What makes these classes different from the general Christian education one receives throughout one's life is not the length or timing of the classes, but their content. The content for confirmation revolves around getting to know the God who has extended the invitation to covenant relationship in this particular place. This is done not only through Bible study but also through learning the creeds, confessions, and catechisms specific to the Presbyterian Church and how the life of discipleship is practiced in this particular local congregation and the denomination as a whole. Confirmands are also given opportunities to speak about their own faith journeys and beliefs as they prepare for the public profession of faith. This brings us to the last part of our definition of confirmation.

Professing Our Faith Publicly

After all the training on what it means to be confirmed in covenant relationship with God and to walk in discipleship with Christ and others comes the moment when the confirmand voices his or her faith publicly. It is not enough just to come to class and memorize the faith of Christian tradition or listen to others' testimonies as to what this commitment has meant to them. One must be ready to voice the commitment oneself if it is truly to be a confirmation of the promises made at baptism.

One activity that I have often done with confirmation classes in preparation for this public profession is to get a sample box of Christian

T-shirts with various expressions of faith on them and then to hang these shirts around the classroom. As the students enter I invite them to look at each shirt and consider which one they would be willing to wear in public and why. As confirmands voice their reasons publicly in class they begin to be aware of what they assent to in their faith that they are willing to share with others. I continue the exercise by asking them to stand by a T-shirt that they would not wear in public and to voice their reasons for this choice, being mindful that the shirt they choose may have already been chosen by another as her faith expression. In voicing their reasons for not wearing a shirt, the confirmands are further clarifying their Christian beliefs as well as being mindful of the diversity of the Christian faith.

Public profession of faith in the formal confirmation ceremony will not involve the visible putting on of a shirt, but will involve the putting on of Christ as a commitment of Christian discipleship. This formal profession takes several forms. It often involves a written personal statement or expression of belief that is shared with the session and congregation. It is also embodied in the answers that are given to the baptismal questions during the service. Finally, it is again reinforced as the confirmands lead the congregation in a recitation of a historic creed of the church, most often the Apostles' Creed. Each of these public expressions convey that this covenant relationship is both a personal and communal journey, that discipleship in Christ involves promises to God and commitment to a way of life that has been followed by many others before us.

As you think about this expression of the meaning of confirmation, consider doing the following:

1. Reaffirm your own baptism by remembering your baptism/confirmation story or by thinking about what these events mean to the faith you have today.
2. Make a list of the commitments to relationships in your life. In what ways is God present in these relationships?
3. Design a T-shirt that you would be willing to wear in public that encapsulates your personal faith in God.

CHAPTER 2

ROLES OF PARTICIPANTS

Ultimately it is not the role of the pastor, teacher, covenant partner, parents, or even the confirmand to determine whether someone is to be confirmed into Christian discipleship. God is the one who invites this relationship. The rest of us may perform the ritual or sign of this covenant commitment, but God has already welcomed the confirmand into the faith community and called him or her by name. However, there are roles for the rest of us during this time, and we will explore these possibilities in this chapter. Even though I have addressed each role to those who fulfill it, it is important to read all the roles to see how the pieces fit together. All are necessary to the nurturing of the Christian community as it seeks to live faithfully and grow into its mission.

Confirmand

If you are reading this section as a confirmand, it must mean that you have agreed to go through special training in preparation for the act of confirmation. Your church may not call you a confirmand, but nonetheless that is your role. In times past you might have been called a communicant, one who was preparing for first communion, but as a Presbyterian of today you have been able to participate with the congregation in the Lord's Supper since your baptism. You may not yet be baptized. If this is the case, you will be baptized directly before you are confirmed and will be able to participate in the Lord's Supper from then on, much as the early church welcomed new adult members.

What does it mean to be a confirmand? In your church it may mean that you have reached a particular age or that you have expressed a desire to join this particular congregation, but it also means that the church is committed to teaching you what it means to be a Presbyterian Christian, to hearing what you believe, and to using your gifts toward the mission of the church. Let's take a look at each of these commitments to which the church has agreed.

Teaching

As a confirmand you will have a series of classes, often at a different time than the Sunday morning education hour. You will study topics such as the creeds and confessions of the Presbyterian Church, including the Apostles' Creed, which you have probably recited in worship. You will look at Presbyterian history (How did this church come to be?). The way Presbyterians make decisions and structure their church government will also likely be a topic. (It may intrigue you to know that our United States government is built on a similar structure, since so many of the founding fathers and mothers were Presbyterians.) There may be other topics that your pastor or teacher will add that are important to your local church: getting to know the members of the session and diaconate, participating in service projects related to your church's mission, sitting in on a committee of the church to see how decisions are made, and learning the structure of worship in your church. All of these are valuable things to learn and will help you to see where you might fit in to the church's mission. They also offer an insider's look about why the Presbyterian Church does things the way it does.

Professing Faith

By far the most important thing that you will do in these confirmation classes is to think about what it is that you believe to be true about your faith and about what it means to be a Presbyterian Christian. Hopefully your pastor or teacher will give you some time in or out of class to begin voicing these thoughts. There are many different ways of expressing your faith. Some people are very verbal and have no problem answering the questions posed in words that leave you saying, "I wish I would have said that." Other people are very logical in their thinking and offer their beliefs in more of a list fashion: "I believe that God created all of us. I believe that Jesus Christ came to the earth to show us God's love and died to forgive our sins." Still others of us have difficulty expressing our faith in words, but can do so wonderfully through art. There are those who sing their faith and those who express the joy of the Lord through dance or movement. Some people have difficulty expressing their faith out loud, but can be very articulate in a personal journal or blog. Others would rather talk to at least one other person face to face and find their faith in relationship with their friends and family. As a confirmand it is your role to find the mode of faith expression where you can most nearly say or profess what you believe. As part of the confirmation process you will be asked to publicly profess your faith in a variety of ways. Individually you will be asked to give a statement/expression of your personal belief to the session and perhaps others. Collectively you will also be required in front of the congregation to answer questions about your beliefs like those asked at baptism. These latter questions are not a test of your knowledge about the topics from your classes, but more like promises that you are agreeing to fulfill in relationship to God and to the church.

In the Church's Mission

This brings us to the other part of your role as confirmand: finding your place within the mission of your particular church and as a Christian in the larger world. How will you live out your vows to renounce sin and evil, turning to Jesus Christ as Savior and Lord in a life of Christian discipleship? The words are familiar in a church context, but how does one actually do this? It may mean giving up bad habits that separate you from God. It may mean thinking about your vocation in terms of how you can best serve Jesus Christ and what God is calling you to do. It may mean getting more involved in the life and mission of your church community by serving others, teaching, or planning worship. Confirmation is not the end of the process in becoming a Christian. It is only the beginning. There will be many choices, many opportunities for prayer and asking for discernment. Christian discipleship may also lead you in places you never dreamed you would go, if you're willing to listen to the God who has invited you into relationship since your birth.

Speaking of your birth, let's take a look at the role your parents or guardians play in the process of confirmation.

Parents or Guardians

You as parents or guardians of the confirmand have the longest lasting human role in the process of confirmation. Many of you have accompanied this confirmand from birth to this point. Through all the changes of growth, school, moving, and changing church leadership, you are the constant in the lives of these individuals seeking a deeper relationship with God. You have modeled what it means to lead a Christian life. For better or for worse, your child has been observing you from birth. You may have had conversations about faith around your kitchen table or at night when bedtime prayers were said. You may have read Christian books and Bible passages together. You may have done some Christian service work as a family, like collecting items for donation or serving in a soup kitchen. First and foremost, your child has observed you in worship and thus has seen his powerful parents or guardians bowing to an even more powerful being. With you he has learned the hymns and songs of our faith, recited the Apostles' Creed and Lord's Prayer, and prayed for the church community.

Families in the Midst of Faith Community

In the course of your worship life as a family you may have also brought this individual before the congregation to be baptized. There may have been family traditions that were a part of this, a particular dress, individuals that were chosen to especially nurture this child, and a celebration following this event. If your child was baptized in the Presbyterian Church (U.S.A.), you also answered particular questions similar to the questions that your confirmand will be asked at the reaffirmation of her baptism in confirmation. Sharing the story of your child's baptism can be one of the ways that you can aid her as she continues to think and claim her Christian beliefs.

This is not a journey that you have taken by yourself, however. In the Presbyterian Church the congregation also takes a vow to nurture those baptized as they grow in faith. Having conversations with your child during this time about the other people who have nurtured him in the faith, and perhaps some of those people from your own life, can show the confirmand that we grow in faith in a community not just as an individual. If you have saved the products your children have made throughout their schooling, now might be the perfect time to pull out those drawings, poetry, and writings that say something about their faith. Seeing what they believed at a younger age may help them to come to terms with where their faith has brought them today.

Four Ways to Help During Confirmation

When the confirmand is in the midst of the special instruction required for this next step in the Christian life, parents and guardians can be of help by showing interest in what their child is learning, having conversations together as the confirmand crafts her public statement of belief, admitting where you still have questions in your own faith, and creating a positive and welcoming relationship with your child's covenant partner. The first two of these suggestions may be self-explanatory. Showing interest in your child's progress and having conversations around difficult projects she has been asked to produce is probably something you have been doing for years during her schooling. Admitting your own doubt may be something new and require an explanation. In continuing a relationship with an unseen God, we are bound to have continuing questions about who God is and how we are supposed to be in community as Christians. To simply repeat the Great Commandment Jesus gave to his disciples of loving God and loving neighbor does not do justice to the many questions that surround this command. We may have restrained these questions in front of our child as he was growing up, but as a confirmand this same child will be asked to wrestle with many difficult questions of faith. Knowing that parents or guardians continue to wonder about these things gives them permission to still wonder even beyond the confirmation ritual and shows them that growing in faith is a lifelong process and not something you attain after a series of classes.

For confirmands, developing a positive relationship with their covenant partner is also important for some of these same reasons. Having trusted persons within the congregation with whom they can ask faith questions they might be unwilling to ask their parents would greatly aid their ability and comfort with expressing their faith publicly. Your knowledge of your child's gifts and strengths may also be invaluable to the covenant partner as she helps the confirmand with incorporation into the mission of your particular congregation. A positive relationship with this person will help ensure that the relationship will continue beyond the ritual, so that your son or daughter can more fully find his or her place in the life of the church community.

Let's now take a look at the role of this covenant partner within the process of confirmation.

Covenant Partner

Sponsoring or mentoring to someone seeking a deeper relationship with God has been a part of the Christian life from the beginning. At a time before the office of clergy was formalized, the sponsor/mentor was the entry for the individual into the Christian community. Think of Philip and the Ethiopian, Peter and Cornelius, Paul and Lydia. During Calvin's time the elders circulated among the family homes within Geneva, helping parents with the cathecetical education of their children and quizzing the children to see how much they had learned. Some of these same historic roles are present in the calling of mentors today.

Faith Conversations

You as covenant partner have a very important role to play in the confirmation process. You are the link between the confirmand and the church community. For better or for worse the quality of relationship you have, the depth of the faith conversations, and the extent with which you are able to be actively involved with the confirmand in various aspects of the mission of the church will say louder than any words you speak what it means to live the Christian life in community. Constancy is key with all of these things. If you have promised to have a conversation on a particular day and time, or have agreed to meet for a particular service project or participate in a confirmation retreat, then the confirmand will expect you to fulfill this commitment. The confirmands too will be asked to make promises and agree to a covenant commitment. What they see modeled is likely to be how seriously they will take their own covenant commitment to the church.

Perhaps some of the reluctance around adults accepting such an important role can be found in the awkwardness of starting any new relationship, particularly a relationship that requires talking about such somewhat taboo subjects as religion and doubt. It may be uncomfortable to begin conversations with "How's your faith today?" So how does one even start this odd yet important relationship? One way to begin is to develop a positive relationship with the whole family, not just the confirmand. Sharing a meal together is a good ice breaker, and the conversation may naturally move to the community that you all share in common, namely, the church. Telling funny stories related to the foibles of the church community or particular great memories you have shared in worship or education may be one way to show the confirmand that church leaders are human too and that the church community is both faithful and imperfect like all groups of Christians. After this initial ice breaker with the family, perhaps a one-to-one time with your confirmand will seem less threatening to both of you. Depending on what you learn about the person you are mentoring, you may want to schedule your next time as conversation time or service time.

If your confirmand seems very shy and quiet during the family conversation, perhaps doing a church mission project together will be a better way to initiate a faith conversation rather than simply sitting together over a soft drink or ice cream. Think about your church's mission and where you are actively involved. What would interest both you and your confirmand? Could you assemble kits of school supplies or serve together in the church nursery or visit a shut-in member or get involved in a building project? Talking about such mission works after they have been performed will often be invitations to a faith conversation.

Another way to approach the faith conversations might be to ask the confirmand to be thinking about specific questions he has always wondered about regarding faith and church. This might evoke fear in you, because you have no idea what might be asked, and so it is difficult to prepare. But it is always permissible to answer, "That's a very good question. I don't know, but let's see if we can work on this answer together." That gives you some time to ask the pastor or other church leaders for resources that you and your confirmand can explore together to gain some insight that will inform both of your faith journeys. The goal of these faith conversations will be to eventually assist the confirmand in crafting an individual public profession of faith that will be presented to the session and possibly the congregation. By this time you will hopefully know some of the particular gifts of your confirmand and can encourage her to use those gifts in the composition and mode of this profession. One of the joys of agreeing to this role is that you too will find your faith being renewed and your baptism reaffirmed, and you may grow to express your faith in new ways within the mission of the church.

Confirmation Day

On the day of confirmation, Presbyterian churches will often have the sponsors or mentors stand behind the confirmands as they reaffirm their baptismal vows, performing the ancient Christian practice of laying hands on their shoulders or heads. This will be a powerful moment for you as you listen to the faith profession of this individual whom you have gotten to know in a variety of ways over the confirmation process. You may be asked to present your confirmand a gift on behalf of the congregation, or you may choose to do this on your own. Appropriate gifts for confirmands include Bibles, hymnals, devotional books, and crosses. You may also wish to give your confirmand a particular object that symbolizes the faith conversations you have had together.

It is important to treat this ceremony not as a graduation service but as an invitation into Christian discipleship as a lifelong process. As we will see in the next chapter, one of the critical needs for the continued nurture of this newly confirmed person is the continuance of this mentor relationship beyond the time of the confirmation process. You may not meet as frequently or have the same type of conversations as before, but the person embarking on a life of Christian discipleship will still have questions and the need of one outside the family with whom to share in Christian service. Again, you are not alone in this process. The pastor or teacher of the confirmation classes can provide training for you and be a resource for your conversations. We now turn to this last role.

Pastor or Teacher

The role of the pastor or teacher during the confirmation process has at least two distinct manifestations. One is the curriculum and teaching of the confirmation training sessions, including the training of covenant partners, and the other is the planning for the actual reaffirmation of baptism service. We will look at each of these in turn.

Confirmation Training Sessions

As we have seen in the history section, the training of confirmands has been mainly the duty of church leaders. In present practice many pastors prefer to teach the classes leading to confirmation themselves. Others involve elders or other gifted teachers in this enterprise. Often in larger churches one pastor will take the lead during the class times, but others will participate in the actual worship service. No matter who actually teaches the class, it is the responsibility of the session to approve the selected curriculum and prepare all who join the church through profession of faith.[1]

What kind of curriculum resource should be used for confirmation? Drawing on our definition of confirmation from chapter 1, we are reminded that confirmation is *the reaffirmation of baptism by a covenant commitment through a public profession of faith.* That being the case, any curriculum resource that we choose or write should draw the learner back to the sacrament of baptism and the promises that have been made by parents or guardians or will be made by confirmands prior to confirmation. It should remind the confirmands that this relationship they are entering into is not a series of facts to be memorized and tested on. The resource should point to God's invitation to this relationship and that even before they were aware of it, God's presence was with them. Finally, still drawing on this definition, the confirmands should be offered many opportunities to begin to express their faith. Looking at the variety of faith expressions in Scripture and the *Book of Confessions* will give them many models to draw on and will show the link between the history of a people and how they talk about their beliefs.

Another thing to keep in mind in choosing a curriculum resource is the needs of the learners. Curriculum should make room for the questions that learners bring to the confirmation process. Resources for addressing these questions include the Bible, the *Book of Confessions*, and *The Study Catechism*, particularly the Confirmation Version. Because confirmands are entering into their covenant commitment within a local Presbyterian congregation, their exploration of the way that Presbyterians make decisions and govern their churches will also evoke questions about how our church compares with churches from other traditions.

Curriculum also needs to make room for the

passionate commitments of youth. What excites your confirmands about their faith, the mission of the church, and a life of Christian discipleship? What activities might be done during the confirmation process apart from classroom instruction that might tap into these passionate commitments? Finally, since confirmation is a beginning of Christian discipleship, practices that ground a way of life should be offered and encouraged as the confirmands begin to think beyond the confirmation process.

Are there curriculum resources that are already written that address this constellation of concerns? The Presbyterian Church (U.S.A.) has several fine options that are flexible enough to lend themselves to many different situations.[2] Each of these current curriculum resources draws on either of the two recent catechisms developed for the Presbyterian Church (U.S.A.). As Presbyterians, drawing on our theological roots from Reformers such as John Calvin, we have returned again to this educational model of questions and answers regarding our faith. Unlike teaching of the Reformation period, however, students are not simply asked to memorize and recite the answers given but to explore both the meaning and the Scriptural sources of these answers. Pastors or teachers who undertake to write their own curriculum for these classes should have an equal theological grounding and focus to their work. No curriculum resource is perfect. All will need to be adapted for the particular setting, teacher, and learners that undertake this journey together. As the leader for this class, be prepared for deep conversations and a chance to reinvigorate your own covenant commitment with God as well.

Let me conclude the curriculum portion of this discussion with a short word on the training of covenant partners. This role is critical in the confirmation process, and those involved should give due consideration to the selection and preparation of those individuals who take on this important commitment. Those chosen should be mature Christians, willing to be open about faith matters and welcoming of the gifts that youth and other confirmands bring to the church community. They should be active participants in the Christian mission and be willing to begin a relationship that will continue beyond the confirmation ritual. Training for these individuals should suggest a structure for their faith conversations with their confirmand and offer both resources for potential questions and strategies to begin and sustain this covenant relationship. You should share with them your expectation of their participation in any retreat or worship participation beyond these conversations, as well as procedures for alerting their confirmands should an emergency arise that precludes their participation during this important time.

This is a great deal to expect to accomplish in the course of confirmation training. It may be why the trend in churches I have worked with seems to be toward lengthening confirmation training from a minimum of eight weeks to as much as a year, culminating in a reaffirmation of baptism service in the spring. The timing of these classes will of course vary depending on the ongoing mission of your church.

Planning the Service

Consideration should be given also to the timing of the confirmation ritual. The early church structured its preparation to culminate in a baptismal service on the night before Easter Sunday, known as the Easter vigil. There are some churches that follow this same pattern today for their services of reaffirmation of baptism. Others choose the prior Sunday, Palm Sunday, where confirmands historically recited the Apostles' Creed, to perform this same service. Some churches make a case for confirming members on Pentecost Sunday, drawing on the earliest baptisms of Christians after the ascension of Jesus at the Pentecost event of Acts 2. Still others, thinking back to Calvin's admonition against a confirmation ritual that would detract from the sacrament of baptism, choose an ordinary Lord's Day in the spring in which to bring these members into the covenant commitment to Christian discipleship. The choice will need to be made by the pastor in consultation with the session.

The *Book of Common Worship* offers several choices of liturgy for the occasion of reaffirmation of baptism. The pastor can choose the appropriate wording and/or can involve the confirmands, parents, or covenant partners in the design of this service. I have often done an overnight retreat for confirmands and covenant partners immediately preceding the day of the service, working through the liturgy so all will understand its meaning and particularly the promises that are being made. Think through how much of this liturgy you will do and which other appropriate individuals to include in the service, such as additional teachers that have been a part of the training, the covenant partners, the parents or guardians, and the confirmands themselves.

Prior to the service, the session will need to be convened for purposes of examining the confirmands' professions of faith. Whether others are invited to this occasion will need to be decided upon by the session, the confirmands, and you. Some churches publish these public professions of faith in the service bulletin on the day of confirmation. Be sure to ask those professing their faith for their permission before setting down their words in print. It may be that some confirmands choose to express their faith to the session through music, art, or oral presentation. If the written statements are going to be printed, you will need to decide how such unwritten statements might be communicated to the larger congregation. One reason to consider making these faith statements public is so that a broader array of the congregation will begin to see these confirmands as individual members of the body of Christ rather than simply as a group of youth or young adults. These statements may lead to further conversations with members outside the confirmation process and help the confirmands more quickly be accepted into the ongoing mission of the church.

There are many other ways that members of the congregation can be involved besides attending and reaffirming their own baptism as these individuals are confirmed. We will look at the ways that the congregation fulfills its baptismal vow of nurturing the individual in our final chapter.

As you contemplate this second chapter, consider doing the following:

1. Read about a role for confirmation that is different from your own role. What does it feel like to walk in another's shoes? What

things can you do to make this person's role easier to fulfill?

2. Consider keeping a journal during the confirmation process to chart your own faith growth, regardless of which role you perform in the process.

3. Plan a common mission project for everyone involved in the confirmation process to participate in. Evaluate this experience with each group after the project is completed.

CHAPTER 3

BEFORE AND AFTER CONFIRMATION

In chapters 1 and 2 we looked at a possible definition for the confirmation process and identified and explored the roles of people most explicitly connected with the ritual of confirmation. In this final chapter, I will make a case for confirmation, not as a one-time ritual in the life of an individual but as a marker on the continuing spiritual journey, a journey that began at the beginning of life and will continue even beyond death. Since only God can know us before our birth and after our death, we must restrict our discussion to the part of life that happens between these events and look for the ways in which the individual is prepared for confirmation and continues his or her life of Christian discipleship beyond this event.

Why is it important to set confirmation in this lifelong context? In a landmark nationwide study of those who had been confirmed within the Presbyterian Church during the height of its membership from the late 1950s through early 1970s, researchers Hoge, Johnson, and Luidens found that of 500 former confirmands surveyed, two thirds of these still claimed church membership.[1] Of this group, two thirds of those surveyed were still Presbyterian, but less than half of those claiming any church membership attended worship more than twice a month. Even more telling for this particular chapter are those who dropped out of church participation at some point after their confirmation. This amounted to 75 percent of the total confirmands, a much higher number than the previous generation. They cited such factors as leaving home, disinterest, church conflicts, and spiritual doubt as being the biggest factors in their decision to leave the life of a church community.[2] About half of those who dropped out returned to a church setting by the time of this survey in the early 1990s.

While these statistics are sobering for those who approach this time of confirmation today, they do not have to be the final word in the nurture we provide to the next generation seeking to profess faith in Jesus Christ. This chapter will explore practical ways that congregations can fulfill their vows made at baptism to nurture children, youth, and adults as they progress on this lifetime relationship with God.

Before Confirmation

Baptism Markers

Relying on our conception of confirmation as a reaffirmation of baptism, the place that we begin the journey toward a public profession of faith is at the font, where the waters of baptism reside in most Presbyterian churches. When families stand at the font, both they and the congregation make vows to nurture the child, youth, or adult in the Christian faith. Often members are reminded of these vows when it comes time to select church school teachers, nursery workers, or vacation Bible school volunteers. These are indeed tangible ways to live out our nurture of children, but are there other ways to remind the individual of the congregation's nurturing care as he or she moves to deeper relationship with God?

Many churches will deliver children's messages during worship around the themes and symbols of the baptism ritual. Often children are invited to get a closer view of the ritual when an infant or child is being baptized. After these services is an opportune time to remember the family stories surrounding children's own baptisms. In some cases older siblings may actually participate in the baptismal ritual of their younger brothers and sisters. This could be as simple as standing with the family at the font, perhaps making a promise to help their brother or sister learn about Jesus, or adding a cup of water to the font. This is another opportune time for the family to discuss previous baptism stories as they make new baptismal memories.

Sometimes churches will give the family a particular gift at the time of baptism. These gifts are often books on Christian parenting or baptismal certificates that can be displayed in the home or placed in a child's book of memories. A church that takes the nurture of families seriously might also assign a deacon or nurture committee member the task of contacting church families on the anniversary of the baptism either by card or phone call. Perhaps a church that would be attuned to the long-term nurture of this child might already assign a covenant partner to this newly baptized member who would agree not only to commemorate the anniversary of the baptism but agree to mentor this child through to confirmation and beyond.[3]

Oakhurst Presbyterian Church in Decatur, Georgia, gives a unique reminder to the family when any infant or child is baptized. At the children's message during the service in which a baptism occurs a pillowcase on a hard backing, inscribed with the date of baptism, is shown. Children, youth, and adults are encouraged to sign this pillowcase after the service as a reminder of who was present at this child's baptism. Also at this same church, as the newly baptized infant or child is introduced to the congregation, the minister talks about the many messages that the world will give to this child, but that the congregation is to remind the child that he or she is first and foremost a child of God. The signing of a pillowcase or the reminder of one's relationship to God are things that all can do within the congregation whether or not they have the gifts and commitment to be a teacher or mentor.

The Home as First Christian Education Setting

Beyond the actual time of baptism there are ways that the congregation can partner with parents or guardians to nurture their children's spiritual development as well as all the other ways they are growing and changing. Children are physically in the church setting for a very small percentage of their week, but in their home for a much larger portion of the time. Since the time of the early church the home has been viewed as the primary place for learning of all sorts, including that of spiritual matters. It is only in recent times that schools have replaced the home as the primary setting of education. The church has rediscovered the home as a setting for Christian nurture and begun to shift the role of primary Christian educator for young children back to the parents or guardians. The church, then, has shifted its role to nurturing and providing resources for parents and guardians in their task of nurturing their children in the Christian faith, as well as continuing to provide supplemental education to children in the church setting.

Some churches have begun Christian parenting classes for this purpose during the church school time or at another time convenient for participants. In addition, many fine resources have been produced in recent years that can guide parents and guardians in the appropriation of such a role as primary Christian nurturer.[4] All of these can add greatly to the confidence that parents and guardians have with regard to nurturing their children's faith.

In addition to these overt acts of creating a home culture that encourages growth in faith matters and inquiry, parents and guardians can also make time on a regular basis to listen to their children's faith expressions or discuss the secondary learning from church school or worship. Some families discuss matters of faith around the dinner table. Others work it into the bedtime ritual at night. Some even carry on a regular family devotional time where the Bible is read and discussed in terms of the family's life experience. This is not unlike the family devotional times during the Reformation when the catechism was also a part of the education of

children. The Presbyterian Church (U.S.A.)
has recently reclaimed this tool as well in the
development of two catechisms, one of which—
Belonging to God: A First Catechism—is especially
helpful for family devotional times.[5] Out of
these family devotional times may emerge a
commitment to a particular Christian service
outside of the home. This modeling of Christian
discipleship may take the form of serving
together in a soup kitchen, assisting an elderly
neighbor with yard work, or traveling together
as a family on a church-sponsored intergenerational mission trip, among many other
possibilities.

All of these ways of nurturing faith in the
home can give children spiritual tools to pursue
a lifelong relationship with God. There are also
ways that the church can pave the way toward an
eventual public profession of faith in reaffirmation of baptism. We will look at some of these
opportunities in the next section.

Nurturing Professions of Faith in Church

One of the ways that children first encounter the
biblical story in community is in the church
school class. In these classroom settings biblical
narratives are heard, enacted, and responded to
in various ways. Sometimes teachers miss the
chance to listen to what children think about a
story and how it influences their faith. This type

of listening is one way that teachers can nurture children toward a public profession of faith.

Here is an example. I was teaching a fourth and fifth grade church school class in southern New Jersey. After presenting the story of the call of Abram and Sarai, I asked some open-ended questions such as, "What do you think Abram and Sarai were feeling when they were told by God to suddenly move to a new place? What did they think of the promise that they would have many children even though they were old and had none?" My questions were met by utter silence. Finally, I saw the proverbial light bulb go off over the head of one of the girls in the class. She said, "Oh, you want to know what *we* think." I realized then that most of the questions we ask of children are designed simply to reassure us that they heard the facts of the story as we have presented it, not to lead them into being biblical interpreters in their own right. If we expect youth and young adults to be able to put their faith in their own language then we have to give children permission to begin to interpret the stories of our faith and link them to their own lives and experience.

Besides asking open-ended questions and making sure they understand the components of biblical stories, another way that the church can help children see their own progress in faith expression is to collect representative samples of their professions and beliefs each year and encourage families to keep these samples as a faith portfolio that can then be brought out during the confirmation process. This technique is borrowed from the art world but is something that many parents and guardians do with school work: saving compositions, exams, and drawings to preserve specific high points in a child's education. The rise in scrapbooking in recent years may be related to this desire to preserve past accomplishments. Written faith expressions, drawings of God or Jesus, or tapes (audio or video) of worship leadership by the child might all be things worthy of preserving in a faith portfolio. Confirmands might then use these previously preserved experiences to gain confidence in publicly professing their faith in confirmation through seeing the growth they have made in their own faith expressions from earlier times. Imagine also the church celebration following the reaffirmation of baptism service when these various faith expressions, in addition to the confirmation profession, are displayed in a fellowship hall or other suitable location for the congregation to get to know the newly confirmed member.

Smaller churches are more likely to know confirmands well. They are more likely to have nurtured these individuals in roles of worship leadership and participation within the church family. In larger churches it can be more challenging to find ways that children can be heard and known to the larger church before confirmation. Rich liturgical planning for the seasons of the church year can often find unique and varied roles for children's faith expressions through banners or displayed artwork, through choirs or liturgical dance, through bulletin cover designs, and through greeting congregants as they enter the sanctuary or church building. There are many ways that children can be nurtured into their roles as full members of the congregation by virtue of their baptism. It is a task in which every committee of the church can participate.[6]

With a rich preconfirmation experience within the home and church, confirmands are well prepared for the process of confirmation and a public profession of their faith and commitment. Many churches respond well to the nurture of the children in their midst. Where churches are less successful is in retaining these newly confirmed youth and young adults after the intensity of the confirmation training and ritual. The next section offers some suggestions for the congregation in order to make the confirmation experience less of a graduation and more of an invitation into a deeper commitment to Christian discipleship.

After Confirmation

After the intensity of the confirmation training and the richness of the affirmation of baptism ritual, there may be a spiritual letdown among those who have participated. Passionate energies may get focused elsewhere as gradually the confirmand becomes one more either active or passive participant in the church's mission. What are some things that Presbyterian congregations can do to keep former confirmands from just slipping away and adding to the number of those leaving the church for other commitments? In this section we will look at two possibilities for maintaining ties with the confirmation experience and then explore the life transitions following confirmation that make it difficult for the congregation to retain ties with those it confirms.

Subsequent Reaffirmation Services

Just as we began the section on congregational nurture before confirmation with the baptismal service, we will begin this section looking at the confirmation process as a yearly cycle in which those who have recently been confirmed may participate with great knowledge and investment within the life of a congregation. This particular idea emerged for me while attending the bar mitzvah of the son of a friend.[7] I noticed that other youth participating in the reading of Scripture seemed to have no particular relationship to the young man but were celebrating the anniversaries of their own bar or bat mitzvahs. Why not then encourage recently confirmed youth to participate in subsequent reaffirmation of baptism services in the Presbyterian Church? In the reading of Scripture, the planning of logistics, or the singing of special music, they can reaffirm their own commitment recently made, as well as serve as models of active Christian discipleship for those who are being confirmed on that day. Using the gifts that were uncovered during their own confirmation process, they can make the day even richer for those who are just beginning to publicly profess their faith in Jesus Christ.

These same youth might also have specific roles to play during the training sessions leading up to confirmation. Perhaps they could rehearse and perform a dramatic portrayal of Presbyterian history for the confirmands. Perhaps they could form a panel to talk about their experiences crafting their own faith statements. Perhaps they could participate in a joint service project with the confirmands, again modeling the living out of the commitment that they made. To prepare the newly confirmed for such roles, they will need to be nurtured into an active Christian discipleship by those who had roles in their confirmation process.

Christian Discipleship beyond
Confirmation within the Church

Dating back to the adult baptism/confirmation process of the early church, the training in preparation for confirmation was not deemed sufficient enough to maintain this personal commitment to a life of Christian discipleship. Even in our earliest written description of the Easter vigil baptismal service by Hippolytus there is a reference to further instruction in the mysteries of the Christian faith. Proceeding to the era of Calvin, education in the Reformed faith did not end when the ten-year-old child was able to recite the catechism; this only marked the beginning of a deeper engagement with Christian theology. Translating this to our present practice as Presbyterians, although the preparatory classes to confirmation will end, this does not mean that all the questions of faith will have been answered or that there will not be deeper theological questions left to explore. Perhaps some of these questions will be raised during the process of confirmation training: Why does God permit suffering? How do Christians relate to those of other faiths? What does it mean to call the church the body of Christ? Where is God calling me to serve in the common mission of the church? Developing a postconfirmation class around these deep questions of faith gives the newly confirmed members some substance for their deeper commitment, a sense that the confirmation ritual is only the beginning of their wrestling with issues of faith.

These questions can be explored in the setting of a church school class or youth group.[8] Another setting for addressing such questions might be in the form of a reunion retreat where individuals could share the meaning that confirmation has had for their continuing faith experience. These questions can also form the basis of continuing the covenant partner relationship beyond the ritual of confirmation. No longer is there the tangible product of producing a public statement of faith, nor the schedule of church-sponsored conversations, yet many confirmands have developed such deep relationships with their spiritual mentors that it is to these people that they would most naturally turn to explore their further questions of faith. The pastor/teacher in the confirmation training process can support this ongoing relationship by providing covenant partners with both biblical references and other resources to aid their addressing of such difficult questions.

Another reason for continuing this relationship with both the confirmands and their families is to ease the transition into the life and mission of church as a newly confirmed member.

Parents and guardians will see gifts within their children that the confirmands may not be able to identify themselves. Sharing these between family and the church member serving as spiritual mentor to the confirmand may help all involved to identify specific ministries both in and out of the church to which the new confirmed member may turn to live out his or her passionate commitment to Christian discipleship. The covenant partner may then be able to find settings for such a living out of these ministry commitments.

Sometimes the church's immediate response to confirmation is to encourage the newly confirmed member to sign up for committee work. In a church where committees are vibrant places of spiritual growth as well as practical mission, this can be an outlet for the commitment made in confirmation. Often, however, church committee work gets so bogged down in the details of running particular programs that the larger mission and faith exploration gets lost. Perhaps a better direction in which to funnel the energies of the newly confirmed is encouraging them to be actively involved in short-term task forces that have a tangible exciting project that can be seen and experienced. Examples include doing worship planning for different seasons of the church year, planning an intergenerational mission project either locally or abroad, or preparing a theologically grounded stewardship campaign for the church.

Active participation in the ongoing mission of the church is certainly one way to retain the newly confirmed, but what will sustain their faith beyond the bounds of the individual church community?

Christian Discipleship in the World

There comes a natural progression in the life of faith when through a move or a change in church leadership or the going off to college an individual may no longer be able to be active in the life of the church community that confirmed him. What then will sustain the newly confirmed member in a world that may not understand or care about his faith commitment? If the youth is simply going off to college and will be home at periodic intervals, the congregation can do many things to sustain her during her education. A regular correspondence through e-mail or handwritten notes between covenant partner and former confirmand will indicate to the latter that she is not forgotten. Asking Presbyterian Women's circles or individual adult church school classes to sponsor a young adult in college through ready correspondence and care packages is another connection. The pastor, using the *PC(USA) Directory*, can readily find a nearby church community to the college the young adult will attend or alert a Presbyterian campus minister of that person's presence at a given college. The pastor can also make a point to reconnect with the students when they are home during break times through a social event, retreat, or individual conversation.

Beyond these practical concrete connections that are made between individuals and congregations, there are other practices that can sustain youth and young adults in this period of letting go. In the field of Christian education there is a growing movement to specific Christian faith practices that can be nurtured into a way to live the Christian life.[9] Emphasizing these practices before, during, and after the confirmation process will offer the individual ways to continue to feed a deeper relationship with God and with our neighbors. Practices such as prayer, discernment, community building, Sabbath, and hospitality give tangible ways of living out a passionate commitment to Christian discipleship regardless of the physical location in which the individual finds herself living out faith.

As young adults reenter a faith community, perhaps at the baptism of their own children, they can be reminded of their own journey from font to confirmation to a life of Christian discipleship as they again make the same promises to nurture their children in the same Christian path in which they have gone before. Perhaps they too will serve as covenant partners for the next generation of confirmands who continue to publicly profess their faith, as they reaffirm their baptism. Through the strength of the congregation's commitment to making the baptismal cycle a central focus of the church community, the Presbyterian Church has a chance to retain those who are confirmed and thereby change the statistical information given on the next generation of Christians. May this next generation be one that clings to the gift of God's grace and love given at birth.

In engaging this chapter consider doing the following:

1. Assess your current church programs. Which are nurturing children, youth, and adults in fulfilling the promises made at baptism and confirmation? How can you make the link between these activities and these rituals more explicit?
2. Begin collecting a portfolio of faith expressions for yourself and those in your family.
3. Choose a particular Christian faith practice as a family or congregation to emphasize over the next year. Set aside some periodic times of reflection and evaluation to assess how this practice is deepening your relationship with God and others.

Notes

Chapter 1: Confirmation

1. The use of the term *covenant partner* is found in James Clinefelter, ed., *Journeys of Faith: A Guide for Confirmation-Commissioning* (Louisville, Ky.: Presbyterian Publishing Corporation, 1996). Some churches use *elder sponsor* or *mentor* to describe the same designated person from the congregation.
2. Theology and Worship Ministry Unit PC(USA), *Book of Common Worship* (Louisville, Ky.: Westminster/John Knox Press, 1993), 447.
3. *The Study Catechism: Confirmation Version* (Louisville, Ky.: Witherspoon Press, 1998), Question 54, p. 35.
4. Two recent curricula along these lines are Chris McNair, *Young Lions: Christian Rites of Passage for African American Young Men* (Nashville: Abingdon, 2001); and Richelle White and Tamara Lewis, *Daughters of Imani* (Nashville: Abingdon, 2005).
5. *Book of Common Worship*, 406.
6. Robert L. Browning and Roy A. Reed, *Models of Confirmation and Baptismal Affirmation* (Birmingham, Ala.: Religious Education Press, 1995), 12.
7. Richard Robert Osmer, *Confirmation: Presbyterian Practices in Ecumenical Perspective* (Louisville, Ky.: Westminster John Knox Press, 1996), 43.

Chapter 2: Roles of Participants

1. *The Constitution of the Presbyterian Church (U.S.A.)*, Part II, *Book of Order* (Louisville, Ky.: Office of the General Assembly, 2005–2007), G-5.0440.
2. There are three resources currently available for PC (USA) confirmation training: Elaine W. Barnett,

Laura S. Gordon, and Margaret A. Hendrix, *The Big Picture: A Resource for Confirmation and Pre-Confirmation* (Louisville, Ky.: Geneva Press, 1998); Emily J. Anderson and Kendy Easley, *Can We Talk? Conversations for Faith* (Louisville, Ky.: Geneva Press, 1998); and Meg Rift and Eunice McGarrahan, *Professing Our Faith: A Confirmation Curriculum* (Louisville, Ky.: Congregational Ministries, 2005).

Chapter 3: Before and After Confirmation

1. Dean R. Hoge, Benton Johnson, and Donald A. Luidens, *Vanishing Boundaries: The Religion of Mainline Protestant Baby Boomers* (Louisville, Ky.: Westminster John Knox Press, 1994), 44–49.
2. Ibid., 53.
3. This role is not unlike the traditional role of godparent but has the distinction of being filled by a member of the congregation rather than a family member or friend chosen by the family. In congregations where geographical mobility is a distinctive feature this may be difficult but not impossible to accomplish.
4. See, e.g., Karen Marie Yust, *Real Kids, Real Faith* (San Francisco: Jossey-Bass, 2004); Elizabeth Caldwell, *Making a Home for Faith* (Cleveland: Pilgrim Press, 2000); and Carol Wehrheim, *Getting It Together: Spiritual Practices for Faith, Family, and Work* (Louisville, Ky.: Westminster John Knox Press, 2002).
5. See Ann Reed Held and Sally Stockley Johnson, *We Are the Family of God: Family Conversations about the Catechism* (Louisville, Ky.: Geneva Press, 1998).
6. Church committees wishing to contemplate the impact of children on their particular areas will be helped by the chapters that address various committee responsibilities in Cassandra Williams, ed., *Children among Us: Foundations in Children's Ministry* (Louisville, Ky.: Witherspoon Press, 2003), 141–95.

7. Bar and bat mitzvah services are the Jewish rituals that occur at about the same age that many youth are confirmed in the Presbyterian Church and also involve a public profession of faith by the reading of Scripture in Hebrew.

8. Although there are a number of resources that explore such questions with youth (the *Questions of Faith* video series and *Becoming Disciples through Bible Study—Youth Edition* to name two), I suggest that churches consider developing their own discussions around the specific questions that arise during the confirmation training sessions. These questions will change from year to year, but there are some perennials to expect, such as the question of God's relationship to suffering and evil.

9. See, e.g., Dorothy Bass, ed., *Practicing Our Faith* (San Francisco: Jossey-Bass, 1997); Dorothy Bass and Don Richter, eds., *Way to Live* (Nashville: Upper Room, 2002); Kenda Creasy Dean and Ron Foster, *The Godbearing Life* (Nashville: Upper Room, 1998).